THE LEFTOVER BROTHER

A Novel

"Such are the prestidigitations of anti-form." Samuel Beckett-Reduction and Apocalypse – The Solipsist Voice.

THE LITERATURE OF SILENCE

By Ihab Hassan

"Atoms are not things. They are only tendencies."

Werner Heisenberg

THOMASINA

Each week I plot your equations dot for dot, xs against ys in all manner of algebraical relation, and every week they draw themselves as commonplace geometry, as if the world of forms were nothing but arcs and angles. God's truth, Septimus, if there must be an equation for a curve like a bell, there must be an equation for one like a bluebell, and if a bluebell, why not a rose? Do we believe nature is written in numbers?

SEPTIMUS

We do.

ARCADIA

By Tom Stoppard

<u>CAST OF CHARACTERS</u>

1 - Morgan............................Physicist, 84

2 - Ben............................ Stockbroker/writer, 35,

                         Morgan's youngest son

3 - Kip........................ Prodigal Son,38, Morgan's oldest

4 - Vivian....................Ph.D. in Mathematics, 33,

                         Kip's fiancee, Ben's wife

CHAPTER ONE

SETTING: STAGE RIGHT - is a section designed to give
the effect of being in an ATTIC, MORGAN's work place
with computer, desk with lamp, with a picture window
view of the HUDSON RIVER, from the West Bank, fifty
miles from NEW YORK CITY. STAGE LEFT is the spacious
kitchen with a round oak table, in the VICTORIAN HOME
of MORGAN, BEN and his wife, VIVIAN. STAGE RIGHT
section is also used for the FOOTBALL PRACTICE, CHURCH,
MENTAL HOSPITAL and BEDROOM scenes.

AT RISE: BEN and VIVIAN sit at table, as sunrise light
steadily illumines the kitchen. After ten beats, Ben
turns, speaks and beckons to the audience.

BEN - All of you out there, if an "out there" really *is*
out there... *come join us!* Step thru the looking
glass, to the entrance of the rabbit hole and see this
drama as a *truth*, but not as a Western abstraction but
as in the Greek *alethes* —becoming unhidden, as a light
flashes into a dark chamber of uncertainty. I'm Ben,
there's Vivian, my brilliant wife of the Zeitgeist.
She's just given me the look she once said she would
never give, the "Oh, it's *still you*" look, irked it's
the leftover brother who's her husband and not my older
bro Kip, who stiffed her at the altar a year ago, then
split for the Coast - the other one. An air of
expectancy piggy-backs the sunlight - do you feel it?
Morgan, my father, the wizard physicist, working in his
attic lab, says the one great story is that we have all
come forth from one ground of being,

as manifestations of time on a timeless ground, a shadow field and we play the game in this shadow field, enacting our side of the polarity with all our might, but all the while knowing our Self is on the other side of our selves if we could only ultimately observe from above the position of the middle. Morgan says we are functions of the carbon atom. I say we must transmogrify or die. Thus, let my play within a play begin.

(Ben opens the New York Times to the financial page as Vivian picks up her coffee cup and sips, then starts, as the doorbell rings and a WESTERN UNION MESSENGER calls out:)

Western Union!

(Vivian rises quickly, goes to the door, returns with the telegram, reads it, sighs, gets a dreamy look, squints out the window at the rising sun.)

VIVIAN -It's him. He's coming home!

BEN - *Who's* coming home? Kip? But how can that be? I thought you said Morgan was launching him into the quantum la la land about now.

VIVIAN - I did. I don't know. Something has happened, maybe Kip has broken the wizard's spell.

BEN - When?

(Vivian tosses the telegram at Ben)

VIVIAN —When...? Well, *there,* read it yourself. I must get his old room ready. (Vivian exists, Ben reads)

BEN – Let's see...arriving this weekend. Today is Monday... so the Cretin will be among us, transfixing my darling but distracted distaff side by Saturday. So it's Kip, not just dropping by for a visit, but a homecoming I knew would happen one day. For this year Vi and I have lived together, I wondered how I would handle it and I'm surprised and pleased that I can focus on the up-side of Kip busting in, like a bull in a china shop - that it inspires top grade drama, a creative reprise of the Biblical myth of what happens when the Prodigal Son comes home to find his father still stuck in the afternoon he'd fled the marriage scene, holed up in his attic using that event to provide a breakthrough into his whacky world of quantum mechanics, finds the ultra-smart, gorgeous girl he'd jilted, married to his younger, leftover brother?

(Lights go down, STAGE LEFT. Sounds of football player's bodies impacting, shouts of players and coaches ring out at football practice. Lights go up, STAGE RIGHT, shows several rows of bleachers where Vivian sits. Ben walks into the action, speaks to the audience.)

BEN – Here you see a typical scene from our collective college memories. There's Vi, dressed in that ridiculous cheer leader's outfit, wearing Kip's letter sweater, great tits out, with a rah-rah grin on her face, dutifully watching and clapping, at her super jock tailback, hippin' and rippin', going "flat out" as he loved to say, running over teammates with a kind of primitive glee. Vivian was, from day one, the class math genius and I was the lit king, destined, it said in our yearbook, to "write up the world". For years I'd been in love - or at least in lust - with Vivian, fantasized over her, projected us into erotic postures such as those coming up in the Rector's office. But here, only our minds did a kind of intellectual coitus, as it were, where she and Kip, I'm sure, were actually fucking. But then they were college King and Queen, pinned at the hip, in sorority speak. Here, no joke, she will be explaining to me Einstein's Special Theory of Relativity, one eye on her lover guy, running by for a score, arm waving in our direction.

(As Kip motors by, Ben takes a seat beside Vivian, grins and fixates on her chest.)

VIVIAN - Ben, isn't your big brother such a *great* player? Now, you and Einstein, concentrate on what I say and not on my boobs!

(Vivian closes her eyes, freezes as Ben speaks to the audience.)

BEN - Since Junior High, Vivian has been the class math queen, headed for a Ph.D. at Princeton, everyone knew. We'd have these contests, get a math problem, the ones I took forever to solve, that went like - you are in a motor boat going x miles per hour down-river and you drop your hat in the water and it goes y miles per hour in the stream. In five minutes, if you pull into shore,

how long will it be before your hat floats by? The rest
of us poor mortals would scribble reductive Newtonian
equations. But Vivian would close her eyes, like now,
get that intense look, and in seconds she'd open them
and write down the answer! When I asked her how she
solved it so quickly, she'd smile and say, "Well honey,
you just get in the boat and you *see* the answer!" What
kept me *out* of the boat was all I could see was Vivian,
the result of The Asperger Syndrome they'd discovered
in my youth, a mild version of a functioning autistic
savant, what most literary artists have, the compulsion
to obsess over an internal imperative, which would
serve me well when I segued into the playwright mode.

VIVIAN - O.K. Ah...take two observers, one on the train,
the other on the platform, to illustrate the postulate.
For the person on the platform, it is the train that is
moving. But the person on the train can just as well
suppose he is standing still and the platform and the
whole earth with it are moving past him. Uniform motion
is relative - you can only say you are moving compared
to something else. *Now* do you see Ben dear?

BEN - As usual, all I could see, when this beauty
looked into my eyes and spoke to me was us in *her* boat,
gliding down some sublime river, coupled in sexual
ecstasy, with an empty mind, as Eros swept the
intellect clean of rational thought including Einstein
and his theory of the cosmic chameleon, the time/space
continuum.

(KIP, football helmet in hand, approaches as Vivian turns from Ben and Einstein, and feasts both eyes, bosom fixed at maximum cleavage, on her sweating, Saturday's Hero.)

BEN - And now you'll see a phenomenon that has always amazed and infuriated me. Vivian's whole body morphed into what I called her Ditz Mode, like those odd ducks with multiple personalities who, sometimes, in mid-sentence or in the middle of an allergic reaction, would change personalities so deeply that the rash would vanish! This scene always made me a little ill, so I exit so the love birds can go at it, flat out.

CHAPTER TWO

SETTING: The RECTOR's office in the EPISCOPAL CHURCH
where Vivian and Kip were supposed to have wed. The
ALTAR is just visible through a window. Oil paintings
of past Rectors and Bishops hang on the wall. A large,
red leather couch is across the room from the desk. It
is one year before ACT ONE, Scene One.

AT RISE: Ben, in a tux, sits at the desk, feet up,
drinking a glass of Scotch. Vivian storms in, in her
wedding dress, her eyes puffy and red behind her veil,
from crying, looks at Ben. From the parking lot out the
window, MORGAN, in a limo, is visible and audible,
having a raging fit, raising holy hell, that his oldest
son had not showed for the wedding he had long looked
forward to, to merge his genius genes with those of the
beautiful, brilliant Vivian, to produce the child who
would continue his work on the theory of everything.

VIVIAN - Good *Lord!* What a hell of a day. Is that
Scotch you're drinking? Quickly, give me a double.

   (Ben pours a drink from his flask, hands it to
Vivian, who takes it, goes to the couch, plops down,
kicks off her shoes, tosses the veil, chugs down the
drink, holds out her cup for another.)

BEN - Hey sweetness easy on this stuff, it's 100 proof.

(He goes over and re-fills her cup,goes back to the
desk and sits.)

(Vivian looks to the window to where Morgan is raging.)

VIVIAN - Listen to him, Ben! Your father is going *ballistic* over this. When I left him he had launched into another realm, ranting how he was not only going to disinherit Kip but would do his damnedest to drive Kip totally out of our lives and back into the quantum wave function field. He's that pissed.

BEN - Right Vi, I can hear him. I can understand his rage. He had his heart so set on the two of you getting together and making the next Einstein, the perfect blend of brains and muscle.(a beat) He can't really do that can he -- totally eradicate Kip from the world?

VIVIAN - Normally I'd say, no way. But Morgan has been obsessed with his work lately, of proving that quantum mechanics works in the macro, hard copy world, not just on the subatomic level, a problem that has long stumped the scientific world. We know tons about large objects like galaxies and planets, have scads of data on electrons and quarks, but not much in between, like how cream dissolves in coffee. Plus, Morgan is not a mere generic genius, but a seer, in the wizard class, cut from the same cosmic cloth as his friends Albert Einstein, Niels Bhor and Richard Feynman were.

BEN - Define wizard.

  (She takes a drink, speaks and starts to slur her words.)

VIVIAN - There are two kinds of genius. One is very smart, a kind of super Mensa mentality, who you could be just as smart as if you only knew more.

BEN - You mean like you.

VIVIAN - Well, yes, sort of. But the wizards are the magicians. They invent stunning constructs out of thin air, like Newton, outside his Principia, worked on odd theological theories,in alchemy, the occult,apocalyptic texts, Einstein's Special and General Relativity, Heisenberg's Uncertainty Principle, with Bohr's Complimentarity, to form the Copenhagen Interpretaion of Quantum Mechanics,John Nash's Governing Dynamics, the Equilibrium Theory in Economics. These mystics pluck them from the matrix of creation by a process of discovery that*if* they could explain it to you, it would be totally incomprehensible. John Wheeler, Morgan's friend at Princeton, said there may be no such thing as the glittering central mechanism of the universe. Not machinery but magic may be the better description of the treasure that is waiting with a bearded Merlin waving his wand over the cosmos.

(Vivian is getting looped. She reaches under her gown, takes off her blue garter.)

VIVIAN - Here, let me get rid of this stupid thing.

(She tosses it at Ben, it lands in his drink. He takes it out, shakes it, looks at it fondly, sighs, as if with visions of where it's been, puts it in his suit coat pocket)

BEN — I'll save this. You might need it again someday. The crowd is gone. I paid off the Rector and he said I could lock up.(a beat — he goes to the window and nods) There is our resident wizard in the limo about to leave, no longer screaming but glaring at us. Do you think he sees us? (a beat) Want to split or what? We can go home, change, and I will take you to dinner before you take off for Cal Tech tonight.

VIVIAN — (She stares out the window) That's so sweet of you Ben but let's stay awhile longer - gives me a chance to adjust to this… *mess* of a day.(starts to cry -- recovers quickly)*Stop it Vivian!* That cad isn't worth all this soap opera anguish.(a beat) Yes, Morgan is drilling us with that great, petrifying gaze of his, like a Zen master, a laser shot right out of Bohm's Implicate Order, or beyond. It's like he's in *the damn room*, flooding us with his magic! I've felt this before, in his attic, like a gathering storm, just before his other breakthroughs. He's on to something, I'm sure of it.

 (Vivian turns from the window, chugs down the drink, giggles, turns to Ben at the desk.)

VIVIAN — Come over here, Ben. And bring Big Mama the booze…and succor me.

BEN — Do *what?*

 (Ben comes over and sits beside Vivian, pours them the last of the liquor.)

VIVIAN - You know...succor...like *comfort me!*

(Vivian lets her hand fall on his crotch. Ben blushes, nervous, starts to sweat.)

BEN - Oh...sure...succor...coming right up, so to speak.

(Vivian begins to morph out of the Ph.D. to the DITZ MODE as she had at the football field. She makes a face, sticks out her tongue at the Rectors and Bishops on the wall staring down at them, shoots Ben a loopy grin.)

VIVIAN - Everyone's gone Ben. It's so quiet and kinda holy, just the two of us. I feel better already. Being with you dear has always been a calming affect on me(a beat) Last night at Kip's bachelor party with the *guys*... did he give any hint that he might do this...*thing*...to me?

(Ben stares at Vivian's hand as it starts to fiddle with his fly zipper)

BEN - Ah... he *seemed*...jumpy, drank too much and then asked me for the fat check Dad was going to give you all as a wedding gift. I resisted but...you know Kip when he wants something. I'm sorry Vi, I shouldn't have greased the rails.

VIVIAN - Don't feel bad. You aren't to blame, you didn't know. It *hurts* so now. He just seemed so ready to do the deed. Maybe if we hadn't slept together, if I had held out the cherry on the stick longer. But Lord, what that boy does to my erogenous zone, flat tears it up. But hell, it's a done deal. So…life motors on, eh Ben honey?

(Vivian unzips Ben's pants, and goes into his privates. The lights dim to reflect the arrival of dusk. At the edge of the shadows, the spectre of KIP, in his football outfit, appears in silhouette as Vivian morphs fully into the DITZ MODE.)

BEN - For Christ's sake Vi, what the hell are you *doing*?

VIVIAN - Nothing!

BEN - Nothing? Compared to what? Oh God…oh Jesus, it feels… Vivian, *stop it!* Someone will come!

VIVIAN - Yes, we will as soon as I get you…ah…*there!*

(After a few beats of manipulation and pre-orgasmic moaning, when Ben is fully ready, she pushes him down on the couch, straddles him and they start to make love.)

VIVIAN - Oh, my darling, *this* is what I have been dreaming of all these years of mere lust, now, us here in the Sacred Realm of Holy Matrimony, as the Man said "till death do us part" etc. etc. That's it, you are at my core, my sweet husband!

BEN - What man? (a beat) Oh God, Jesus Lord…I'm coming!

VIVIAN - Yes, dear lover. Let it go, join me in high ecstasy!!

(As Vivian and Ben ,fully engaged, approach climax, Kip
steps out of the shadows, stands watching. As they
reach orgasm, they both shout...)

                    FLAT OUT!

CHAPTER THREE

SETTING: The ATTIC, MORGAN's working space. It is late afternoon.

AT RISE: Morgan is at his desk, staring at his computer. Vivian, in jeans and red turtle neck, sits before him, drinking coffee with one squinting, calculating eye on a white board filled with equations, in the middle of which is the image of a man with the striking resemblance to Kip.

VIVIAN - Morgan, I felt really bad Kip had left me in the lurch at the church but also that I could not talk to you that next morning about that insane day. I had to catch the Red Eye to Cal Tech for a two week teaching gig. That trip was *supposed, to, damn it,* have been our honeymoon. (a beat) I remember that you were in a rage at Kip, and were going to try to take him totally out of our world and place him in the duplicitous world of quantum physics. Were you *serious* about that?

MORGAN - Yes indeed, my dear, serious as sin! The light flashed in on the method on the surge of that rage. What you see on the board is my solution to the macro/micro problem! The experiment is up and running. It was not easy, getting there, it never is, finding the right code to the cosmic lock. But as Einstein always said, the result is elegant and so simple afterward, that a child could understand it. Right now, I'm doing the math.

VIVIAN - Yes, I see what you've done, to a point. My quantum theory is a little rusty. Can you bring me up to speed vis a vis Kip's involvement in your quantum crusade?

MORGAN - Sure - but first, that afternoon at the church, how did you and Ben handle the debacle? You all stayed on at the church?

VIVIAN - Yes, we saw you looking at us after your rant. Ben and I, as we have over the years during the rough patches Kip is so good at stirring up, talked it out. Ben was such a comfort with his calm words of reason. In fact, we made some plans of our own. Maybe with Kip gone we could make a relationship work; dear friends first, then lovers later? He certainly is the sweetest albeit the safest of... men, Kip's polar opposite, thank God for small favors!

MORGAN - Well, that's certainly a possibilitiy?

VIVIAN - We're making a real effort at putting together something positive out of the wreckage Kip left behind him as usual. (a beat - gets up and looks intently out the window at the stretch of the Hudson River leading south to New York City) Now, why don't you give me the details of your breakthrough into the micro/macro mystery that started at the church and how it relates to what Kip did.

MORGAN - OK, I'll give you, in sequence, the data and background, so you can *see* the picture as it appeared to me.(a beat) You know of the invisable wall between the macro and micro worlds, between Newtonian billard ball physics and the slippery world of particle physics, the realm of superposition,what Johnny Wheeler calls a smokey dragon?

VIVIAN - Yes, the course in Physics 101 I took from your friend John Wheeler at Princeton is returning.

MORGAN - *This* is the space into which I'm placing Kip, and began that process in a burst of mind-light at the church. Here, an object can be in two or an infinity of places at once, and as either a wave or particle depending on how it is measured.

VIVIAN - But not at the same time, right? Isn't that what Neils Bhor added with his complimentarity?

MORGAN - Indeed he did - to complete the Copenhagen Interpretaion of Quantum Mechanics, fleshing out Heisenberg's uncertainty principle which is generally understood to be, the more you know about one half of the electron, as its speed, the less you know about the other half - its position, and vice-versa.

(Morgan picks up a piece of paper from his desk, hands it to Vivian)

MORGAN - Like that picture. View it from one angle, it's a crone. Change your angle of vision and it becomes a beautiful girl. This picture comes as close as we can to understanding quirky superposition. The rigid Newtonian eye will *never* see that subtle shift.

VIVIAN - Now about Kip's tumble into superposition…?

MORGAN - You knew I was working on the micro/macro puzzle. Why, in the subatomic cloud of possibilities, could electrons be at two or more places at once? Could that happen with macro objects and if not, why not? At the church I was at critical mass as Einstein was on his trolley car when he saw the Bern clock tower, where Heisenberg was as he stared dumbfounded into his cloud chamber, when special relativity and the uncertainty principle burst out of paradox, and turned the laws of physics topsy-turvy.

VIVIAN - Like can your car be parked at two places at once in superposition? Didn't Schrodinger shed some light on that area, using matter waves in locating an electron, with his famous cat in the box paradox and thought picture?

MORGAN - Yes, he devised the central equation on holiday, when he took time from his Dark Lady of Arosa… Erwin was quite the ladies man…to do the math. But then Born shot down his wave mechanics as not being problem specific, said that it only proved the *probable* location of the electron.

(Morgan goes to the white board, carefully adds some numbers to an equation above Kip's image, turns and sits back down.)

MORGAN - Erwin, disgusted he'd lost his lovemaking time, as a joke on uncertainty, came up with his Schrodinger's Cat paradox. Until you *look* into the box, the cat is alive *and* dead. Not *really* but here we have a threshold view of superposition - one car, in two parking spaces.

VIVIAN - But how does the car muscle in for its place in the realm of quantum superposition?

MORGAN - Aye, there's the rub. There have been recent experiments to show superposition can exist in the macro world. Lukens and Friedman in New York, instead of a cat, used a small square loop of superconducting wire for the direction of the flow of electric current, clockwise around the loop or counterclockwise. They measured the energy to assure that the current was not just flipping but existed in a true quantum superposition. There have been other experiments to show how large objects can be split into superposition.

(Vivian looks back at the white board, and the figure of Kip)

VIVIAN - I see where you are going with this, and how your method emerged at the church under the power surge of your rage at Kip - how to reduce a large object to the double or even infinite states in superposition?

MORGAN - *That* task is what I attacked after my vision at the church. What keeps large objects blocked from the fuzzy realm of superposition is the villain in our drama - decoherence - where the continuous jiggling against the surrounding environment nudges objects out of the blur of quantum potentia into a Newtonian object. Pearle in Italy proposes that we add a term to Schrodinger's equation, that, in effect, constantly jiggles the fabric of the universe. Micro objects only jiggle a little and thus remain a blur, which preserves the predictions of quantum mechanics. Macro objects, like people and the Moon, jiggle more and quickly, and fall into a definite state, which corresponds to everyday existence.

VIVIAN - So by removing decoherence, an object, like a certain *person* we both know, can be coaxed into a quantum blur, *inside,* then in a quantum leap, *outside* the box!

MORGAN - *Precisely! Now* do you see the picture I saw at the church? And how I used it to solve the macro/micro problem? The thought picture is always crucial in these discoveries, the most famous being Einstein seeing a motorcycle cop chasing a light beam but never catching it. And Heisenberg shining a light on an electron in his cloud chamber, and changing a wave into a particle.

(Vivian takes the laser pointer and puts the red line on the board on Kip's face - turns it a glowing red.)

VIVIAN — Well done, wizard! You took Schrodinger's cat out of the box and inserted, sans the major hard copy jiggle, Morgan's first born son. Bravo! You know Morgan that the discovery of your method of stripping, at will, decoherence from macro objects, if you bring this off down the road, a Nobel is pretty much a slam dunk.

MORGAN — A Nobel from all this would be something. And I've kept it all in the family. Kip and you didn't marry and produce my new Einstein, but this is even better, don't you think?

VIVIAN — Well yes — and no. Let me play the devil's advocate. Yes, in the sense that if you win a Nobel for this breakthrough of great magnitude, you'll be placed in the firmament of the leading physicists of our time, right up there with Bohr, Heisenberg, Schrodinger, Feynman, and Nash and Godel in math. And it *would* be in the family as you say with Kip as your avatar of invention. And the award is substantial. But maybe no, in the sense of where do the twin Kips *go* after Kip is re-sectioned? How do you know they won't be sent to wander the world of quantum ghosts? Or worse, be sucked into some black hole? What price scientific fame and fortune?

MORGAN - Not likely - what *is* likely, the probabilities are that he...they...will be sent into a benign parallel universe perhaps by way of teleportation that Zeilinger has proposed. In quantum law, though the *location* of an electron may be uncertain, the probabilities in an infinite universe, are anything that *can* occur, *will* occur. String theory has gone from a theory of everything to a theory that almost anything is possible. Murray Gell Mann holds that everything not forbidden is compulsory. A particle takes all the paths it can and what we see is the weighted average of all those possibilities. That pointer, quantum law says you leave it there long enough, it'll fall through the table!

VIVIAN - Like a monkey pounding away at a typewriter for infinity. He will eventually write Hamlet. Kip and his doppelganger, will *probably* end up in a benign world. *Probably* being the operative word here, not for sure. So when is the execution date, when are our golden "boys" set to sail into the cosmic sea with the Flying Dutchman?

MORGAN - Execution is a bit harsh. Sacrifice might be a better term for it, if you look at it as a kind of quantum entanglement assisted transport of Kip's vital data to another digital dimension. What is sacrifice? The verb, from the latin: sacer + facere, means to make something sacred, by offering, relinquishing or destroying. To be made sacred is to be rescued from utility. And Kip *is* Mr.Utility.

VIVIAN - Kip sacred? That's a bit of a stretch. But aren't you playing God here or as Einstein would say "playing dice with the Universe", relying too much on chance that the dynamic duo will live on outside the box, in your unverified version of a multiverse? Or acting out of anger and not science? At the church, I was as furious as you were at the jerk and what he did. *But that's Kip!* If you'd asked me then, if Kip should be zapped into outer-space, I would have said, goddamn well *do it!* But look what that rage has given you,a *probable Nobel!*

MORGAN - Well, yes but I must stay in the big picture. As David Finklestein asked, "Which are we to build out of our quanta, beings or becomings, essences or existences?" *I* choose to do *this* with my first blood.

VIVIAN - Well, your call. I guess. I have to go. Ben is taking me to dinner, doing some serious courting.(a beat) Now with Kip… when…?

MORGAN - We found him in Laguna Beach, California. I have operatives working helping with the process. We set him up with a girlfriend Carla, and some friends, Cole and James.In a year,he'll be ready for lift off.

VIVIAN - The process is not painful I hope.(a beat)Then ETD is a year - give or take?

MORGAN - Yes, give… or… take.

CHAPTER FOUR

SETTING: The KITCHEN with round table, the morning after the morning Vivian and Morgan met and talked in the attic.

AT RISE: Vivian has on Ben's red robe. Ben is in a white one, inhaling a black Espresso, appearing bleary eyed and worn down as if he'd spent the night suffering the Chinese water torture. They sit vis a vis at table.

VIVIAN – Ben, honey, I really had a great time last night, with the dinner and the dancing. But I'm afraid I drank too much…and got a little… *frisky* when we got home. I'm sorry I got you all worked up but we stopped just in time, didn't we? Aren't you glad we quit before…you know…and we talked most of the night?

BEN – Right, Vi, I'm down-right *ecstatic* we quit groping and I got to talk in bed with the beautiful girl I've been lusting after since grammar school, lying beside me half dressed.

VIVIAN – Oh, Ben, you're so *funny!* But I think it would be sweet and unique if we waited for our wedding night for sex. I don't want to, not yet at least, turn *this* affair into a fuck fest like I had with your brother.

BEN – Good heavens, by all means, let's not let *that* happen!

VIVIAN - So how did you and Morgan get along when I was at Cal Tech? I hated to leave so early after our nice… *chat at* the church, what we talked about for our future.

(Ben turns to the audience with a look of utter disbelief.)

BEN - *Chat,* Vivian? That's a strange name for it! You don't really remember what we did, do you? Good lord!

VIVIAN - (she gets up for more coffee, kisses Ben on the cheek) Remember what, dear? (a beat)You know, Ben I really *missed* you. I thought of you often.

BEN -(takes her hand and kisses it) Did you: likewise my dear, brainy girlfriend. (a beat) I hardly saw Dad, after we came back from the church. But I could hear him working all night, talking to himself, or to someone on the phone. Tell me, how did get along with him yesterday?

VIVIAN - It was most amazing. You remember in his rage at Kip at the church he said he was going to eliminate Kip from the world of the living? Well, brace yourself. Apparently he's doing it and will probably win a Nobel prize in the process! His work would be a fantastic invention, the most advanced since particle superposition was conceived.

BEN- My God, you're kidding. (a beat - he looks at Vivian) No, you're *not* kidding. How in the world did he manage *that?*

VIVIAN - I told you Morgan was working on the macro/micro problem, and how to make macro objects, exist in the micro world, in quantum potentia, called the state of superposition, in more than one form. As we speak, *we* are macro objects. What keeps us together, as it were, and not floating around in a quantum flux, is that our electrons smash against our surroundings at a very high rate that knocks us out of superposition. We jiggle more than quantum beings. That is called decoherence. Morgan at the church in his search for the way to eliminate decoherence, and have large bodies enter the world of superposition, was at critical mass. He was right at the edge of seeing the thought picture that would push him over, when Kip bailed. Morgan's rage at that was the trigger to forcing that quantum leap. And as a mother giving birth, gives her baby the final push into our world, Morgan made the final push into the way to eliminate the decoherence around Kip and send him into another realm. Morgan says that in about a year Kip, who is in Laguna Beach…

BEN - *Where?*

VIVIAN - Laguna Beach, California. That's where Morgan said Kip is, and where Morgan is working his quantum magic on him.

BEN - *Jesus H. Christ!*

VIVIAN - Quite! Morgan says that in about a year the process will have run its course and your flakey brother and my ex main squeeze will have made the supreme scientific sacrifice and sent packing.

BEN - But isn't that *way* over the top? Kip was a major jerk but to do *this* to him? Is Dad that vengeful?

VIVIAN - No, he isn't and I think *that* is starting to wear him down. He was in a rage when Kip didn't show but as I reminded him yesterday, playing the Socrates, that if it were not for what Kip did and the rage it engendered, he would not be in a position to maybe take home the glittering prize in Stockholm. Morgan is in a double bind, a devastating dilemma. He has experienced what theoretical physicists live for - a tsunami moment when he knew something that nobody else has ever known, a revelatory flash of a new glimpse into what Einstein called the Mind of the Old One. He would be a physics legend in his own time. But *behind* that is the shadow side- that his son, *without his consent* will be sacrificed for the gods of science. He's between a rock and a hard place.

BEN - So what do you think will happen?

VIVIAN - We should know in about a year when Kip will be ready to be shot into Showtime. The prize is so *huge* here Ben, and Morgan has convinced himself that when the hammer comes down and Kip is fully into the quantum flux, existing as two forms of the same body, he will be shot into a benign parallel universe that we all might end up in some day. I think now, with what is entailed with winning the Nobel Prize in Physics, the odds are that Morgan will roll the loaded dice. But…?

CHAPTER FIVE

SETTING: Late night in Morgan's attic workshop.

AT RISE: Morgan sits at his computer. He is speaking on a cell phone.

MORGAN - Carla, yes. I got your message that everything has been done and we are at critical mass with Kip. He is at fail safe now and all I have to do is activate the circuit to send him into his new world. You have done a great job in this and I will get you a nice bonus for you and your crew. Goodbye and good luck.

(He turns off the phone, looks at his white board)

Well, at least it *could* have worked. But ever since Vivian questioned my numbers, serious doubts have been building up - too heavy on my mind. *I just can't risk it!* I'll write Carla to shut down the project, to re-program Kip to come home.

(Morgan sits at computer and types)

MORGAN - After all, bottom line, blood *is* thicker than physics.

CHAPTER SIX

SETTING: At the round table in the kitchen. It is the next Saturday after Ben and Vivian got the telegram that Kip was coming home.

AT RISE: Ben and Vivian sit at the table. Vivian stares out the window, her face set in distress, picking at her food. Ben puts down the New York Times.

BEN - Well, love of my life, are you ready for the homecoming of our very own Prodigal Son?

VIVIAN - I *was* ready, in spades, hot to trot when we got the telegram. But I've been thinking it through Ben, from all sides and angles, tossing and turning all night in my bedroom, and I'm terribly conflicted by it.

BEN - Tell me about it!

   (Vivian rises, gets more coffee and pours more for them, walks to the glass door to the garden patio.

VIVIAN - Well, it's two things, actually. Assuming Morgan's decoherence machine is still cranking, it is about time for Kip to blast off from Laguna Beach to out yonder yet he is about to be here. What has happened? Has Kip broken free of Morgan's magic? But we can't take the chance if he is about to nail his Nobel, and take Kip in. If Kip is in the final phase, we *look* at him it's like collapsing the wave to a particle and

Morgan's shot at the Nobel is history. Morgan is so fragile now and the shock of the loss might do him in, push him into a madness like John Nash. Can we risk that being on our conscience? I think not.

BEN – And the other reason?

VIVIAN – It's how we have...*progressed* in our marriage. I know I promised I wouldn't, if we married, look at you as a kind of second fiddle, leftover brother, that I lost Kip and I was settling for you as the runner up.

BEN – Until recently you've been pretty good about keeping your word on that.

VIVIAN – But *pretty good* is not good enough, I decided last night. You... we... the holy state of matrimony, our marriage vows deserve more. The first thing I thought of when we got his telegram was I would soon be in the arms of my great lover, and morph as you say I do into a sex fiend Ditz. So what happens if he comes home? I stay in high dudgeon, that he left me at the altar, then we make up, and we screw our brains out. That orgy goes on for, say, a week, or two, just to get him out of my system...a month, max...

BEN – *Enough already!*

VIVIAN – Quite right! And then too, *we* lose what we've built up this past year, a good, solid life, a bit boring around the edges but getting better, getting close to having that baby we and Morgan want. I just can't do it, though it will be torture to resist Kip.

BEN — So what do we do when he shows up?

VIVIAN — Just don't let him in! Don't *look* at him, as if he is still in the process that would destroy his full entry into superposition,and Morgan's great prestige as the physicist of the age dissolves…

BEN — And my prize as well..

VIVIAN— Yes, and yours too —all slip into gone forever.

BEN — But there's a downside to keeping Kip out of our lives. I was really looking forward to seeing how this was all was going to play out, the dramatic story of what happens when a Prodigal Son comes home to find a family such as ours, with his father stashed in the attic, an obsessed physicist and the girl he jilted married to his younger, sort of wimpy, leftover brother, then write it up as a play.

VIVIAN — *Not so!* You are always saying how you wanted to get back into writing, as you did in college, said if you only had a great story line to get you started. Well, here it is in blueprint form. Just write up what *would* have happened if Kip *had* gotten in here, stepped out of Morgan's decoherence drill. You can set up in the den. I'll guard against interruptions, keep you all comfy in your creative cocoon until you finish!

BEN — Yes, I'll get out all my writing books, delve into my well-worn copy of Esslin's - The Theatre of the Absurd, find my old Selectrix, and writer's duds. And you can be my Muse. Any ideas on a working title?

VIVIAN — Why don't you call it The Leftover Brother?

BEN – *Great* Vi, you are just too much! I can't wait to get started. Even as we speak, I'm *seeing hot* scenes that I want to put in LOB. They are appearing on my inner Asperger screen of internal imperatives. (a beat)It feels *great* to get into the exciting life of a literary artist, now that I have something to write about.

(The doorbell rings…rings…then a banging on the door)

BEN – It's *him*, Vi, Just hold on tight. It'll be over soon. The Ditz will come and go. And our new life can begin. Let's go upstairs and start work on our new baby. And dream when Morgan is a legend in his own time, his Nobel Prize is in the oven as well as his grandchild.

CHAPTER SEVEN

SETTING: Morgan's attic space.

AT RISE: Ben sits at Morgan's table typing on an IBM Selectrix. He is thinner, with longer hair, in jeans, black turtle neck, and cowboy boots. It is two weeks after ACT TWO, Scene One. Ben types hard and fast, finishes with a flourish, turns, speaks to the house.

BEN – *There!!* I'm done for the day, pleasingly written out yet leaving a little in the well, in fine Hemingway fashion. Now some food, a nap,and back at it. You might be surprised to see me and not Morgan here working. Since my darling spouse made that brilliant suggestion that I write up the fictional tale of Kip's homecoming, I've been here since, sleeping here, obsessed as Morgan was on *his* quantum quest, writing my play, The Leftover Brother. On a sad note though, when we kept Kip out of our home and lives, thinking to let him in would ruin Morgan's chance at a Nobel, and our marriage, we didn't know that Morgan had shut down his project and programmed Kip to come home, a *real* Prodigal Son. When Kip couldn't get home, Morgan cracked and we had to commit him to a top grade mental hospital. I plan to visit him tomorrow, to tell him about my work on LOB.

CHAPTER EIGHT

SETTING: STAGE RIGHT is a MASTER BEDROOM

AT RISE: Kip and Vivian are in bed, under the covers, having sex. Vivian is on top, in a tee shirt. She climaxes loudly.

KIP - Not so loud darlin'- Ben might hear you.

VIVIAN - Not to worry. He's sealed up in the attic thinking he is writing all this up, what he *imagines* would have happened had you broken through Morgan's quantum wall.

KIP - Damn, we'll be in the Guiness Book of World fucking records if we keep this up. You know, I still can't get over the fact that Dad was so mad at me that he put me in some kind of quantum swamp in Laguna Beach, and was prepping to deep six me.

VIVIAN - Your no-show slammed Morgan hard. After the initial rage triggered the chain of events, his drive became automatic, a runaway train, a foreign, almost demonic force took control, an engine of obsessive discovery. Any personal intent became impersonal. Once a seer of Morgan's caliber, right up there with Einstein, gets going, they become ruthless, obsessed, desperate and the precious process takes on a life of its own. One cannot tell the dancer from the dance.(a beat) So you started feeling bad eight months ago?

KIP – Yeah, it was like a flu bug. I started feeling weak and disoriented. It drove me *nuts*. Doctors couldn't find a cause. Two months ago, it really got bad.

VIVIAN – You had reached critical mass.

KIP – Then when I was about to check out, thought I was a goner, that next morning after a deep sleep, it left like magic.

VIVIAN – It wasn't *like* magic, it *was* magic. Morgan shut it down, then called off the dogs.

KIP – Dogs? What dogs?

VIVIAN – Morgan had some help, some operatives keeping you in line. A Carla, and two guys - Cole and James.

KIP – *Get back!* Not Carla Bell! And Dad was doing all this from that attic where Ben is now, with some voodoo physics? Good God.

VIVIAN – Then he started you heading home. But when we kept you out, and he saw it from his attic, he cracked and we had to commit him to the Seventh Heaven Mental Hospital and Spa for observation and treatment.

KIP – Then you hunted me down and brought me home. You saved my life, Vi. I was a heartbeat away from disaster.

VIVIAN – But first I had to do something with poor Ben. I wasn't going to let you get away again, big guy.

KIP – How was it being married to little brother?

VIVIAN — Ben is all right, but, bottom line, an underachieving loser. Maybe he'll get some stones like you by writing his play. He seemed lit up by the idea.

KIP — What is it called again?

VIVIAN — The Leftover Brother.

KIP — Strange title.(a beat) It's awesome the way you got Ben to start writing it and that he *thinks* we are together only in his play. How did you pull *that* off?

VIVIAN — Ben was always whining how he hated being a stockbroker, wanted to write. He was driving me nuts. Before you arrived, to clear the way for us to connect, I suggested he hole up in the den and write full time. Then he moved to the attic when when Morgan was committed. He's in another world and we have...*this!*

(KIP cocks his head to hear Ben typing.)

KIP — Is that Ben typing ?

VIVIAN — Yes, but ignore it. That way we know he is still busy in his fantasy world.

KIP — Now, tell me again how Ben's commitment today is going to work. I don't want any screw-ups. I want Ben out there with Dad. That typing makes me nervous, and a little…*queasy* like I did with Dad's weird quantum hex. You're sure Dad can't start that up again?

VIVIAN — Morgan is one worn out wizard. With Ben, I got commitment papers based on our sworn affidavits that he is obsessed in his attic, stays there 24/7, writes all the time, hears voices and thinks that we are here only as characters in his play. And when I told him that I had found you and let you back in, that I wanted a divorce so we could marry, he cracked like Morgan.

KIP - You told him I was here?

VIVIAN - Yes but he refused to believe it. He was so far into his obsession that you only existed in the play, that he blocked it out- stayed in his delusion.

KIP - You're sure that's enough to get Ben locked up? What you said Ben does, isn't that what *all* writers do?

VIVIAN - Sure they do but to Crises Center people, context is all controlling. A New York City shrink, in order to test the levels of insanity it would take to commit, sent a bearded, Bohemian writer into a psych ward intake with those "symptoms" and he was locked up on the spot.

KIP - If you say so. I just hope it works.

VIVIAN - We'll soon have the house to ourselves. (a beat) Quick - let me give you complimentary hummer.

(Vivian dives under the sheets, starts in, Kip starts moaning when the doorbell rings. Vivian comes out and looks around.)

VIVIAN - Oh *shoot!* It's the deputies come for Ben. Let's get this done, get Ben settled in at the funny farm with his Dad, and get back here and go flat out!

CHAPTER NINE

SETTING: Morgan's ROOM at the Seventh Heaven Mental
Hospital and Spa.

AT RISE: Morgan sits in a chair, staring out the window
into a dark, stormy day, with thunder and lightning
strikes, with the dead eyes of the catatonic. Ben sits
beside him, speaking to him - *sotto voce*.

BEN — So... Dad...Vivian sends her love and said to tell
you she talked to the Nobel man and assured him that
your breakdown is only temporary, and if they want to
consider you for the prize, you could attend the
ceremonies in Stockholm. Great news, eh Dad?

(Ben waits for any reaction in Morgan's face but
there is none.)

BEN — But the best news is I've had a huge breakthrough
in my writing. As I told you when we kept Kip out of
the house, we didn't know you had shut down the show,
that it was you who sent him home and you cracked, Vi
had suggested I write a play about what *might* have
happened had Kip returned which I am doing, writing in
your attic space. The writing is going so well that I
thought it was just because I was sitting in your
genius seat. But this morning as I stared at the white
board of the equations with Kip's photo in the middle,
I had a major insight--that the creative matrix

that produced *your* breakthrough, is the same source
that gives *me* the pictures, the hot scenes in my play!
Art and scientific discovery come from the same source!
And that you've channeled your genius power to me. So
we have killed two birds with one stone. You can still
get your Nobel because Kip is for that purpose, still
out there in your blur. Yet I can bring him "back" for
you in my play, which you can read when you get out.

(The storm passed, a ray of sunlight hits Morgan's
face and he grins.)

BEN - *Great Dad!*, you've come back as we knew you
would. I'll tell Vi the great news. I've got to run.
But keep sending your creative energy to me!

(Ben goes to the intercom and presses the button.)

BEN - Nurse Jones, *great news*! Dad just had a
breakthrough moment out of his catatonia! Can you come
down and let me out? I have to meet my wife for lunch.

NURSE JONES (over the Intercom) Now Ben, you know I
can't do that. You keep trying this when you know you
were committed last week when your wife and brother
testified you had lost your mind, that you wouldn't
believe she left you and will marry your brother, and
you insist they are only together in your play. Now go
back to your room and stop bothering your father with
foolish ideas of recovery or we'll put you back on the
thorazine.

CHAPTER TEN

SETTING: The kitchen and round table, as before.

AT RISE: The scene is the same as ACT ONE - Scene One only Kip is where Ben was. Kip tosses a football from hand to hand, dressed in his old football jersey and gray sweat pants. Vivian, where before she was refined and coiffed, is now a slob, hair in red, plastic curlers, sans make-up, in a ratty pink robe, a lit Camel cigarette hanging from her lips, reading the comics in the local rag.

KIP - (full of himself) Vi, could you please not smoke at the table? Thanks. *Damn,* I feel good today, really happy at how things are going for us. Say, did I tell you that me and some of the old football gang are getting together this morning and forming some teams for a tackle league? Butt some heads. I really miss smashing into people, on a dead run, good for the soul. You can come and watch, like the old days. Remember?

VIVIAN -(takes a drag, coughs, stamps it out) Yes, I remember. (a beat) How come you left me in bed this morning before we had our usual morning fuck?

KIP- Went out for a run. I need to get in shape, after that ordeal in California, and I'm getting love handles. Besides, I'm a little sore and a tad worn out. We've been going real heavy on the hard sex.

(Vivian takes a notebook and compact from her wicker purse, and writes in the book, recites, *sotto voce*)

VIVIAN - Too tired and sore to fuck!

KIP - What are you writing? You never write anymore. Why now?

VIVIAN - Certain things have to be noted.(a beat- she looks into the compact mirror) Good God, I look ghastly.

KIP - You look fine to me. As I said things are going well except why did we have to take Ben back and let him stay up there in Morgan's old attic space?

VIVIAN - Well, he was out in the loony bin for a month, and he got a lawyer to spring him. But he was a basket case, would have been homeless if we didn't take him in. Besides, he's so loaded up with meds, he's harmless

KIP - Well, at least he doesn't type anymore. That typing was driving me bonkers, not just the sound but it was like drilling holes in my brain. I began to feel as I had when Morgan was waxing me in Laguna.

(Vivian takes the curlers out of her hair.)

VIVIAN - I'm off to the beauty salon for a complete makeover.

KIP - What the hell is a complete makeover?

(From the attic, comes the sound of typing. Kip looks up at it nervously, starts fuming.)

KIP - What the fuck is *that* Vi? Ben has started typing again. *Christ!* I thought it was a condition of his return that he was not to type, and work on that stupid play where we only exist here as the characters.(a beat - the typing gets faster and louder) Damn it, I'm getting the sick to my stomach feeling again that I got in California when Dad was hexing me. I had a nightmare last night that all that came back again but worse. Can't you go up there and make Ben stop it?

VIVIAN - I could but that typing keeps him busy. And Morgan, though he's getting better at Seventh Heaven, bottom line, is burned out. Your nausea might be psychosomatic, from the guilt of what you did to Ben, seducing and stealing his wife, sending him to the cuckoo's nest.

KIP - Guilt Vi? It was all *your* idea, sending him to the attic to write his crazy play, then to the asylum. And if Morgan isn't the one who's capping me, who the hell is?

VIVIAN - I have no idea -probably no one. I'm outta here. Try and relax. Go play football. It's all in your head.

(As the typing gets louder and faster, Kip begins to shake, sweat, panic and paces the room, staring at his hands.)

KIP – Sure, it's all in my head. Where the fuck *else* would it be? Don't leave me. I need you to hang on to. I'm losing my grip, starting to fade out like before!

(Vivian is gone. Kip runs to the mirror on the wall, examines his face, as if it is receding into the glass, then shakes his fist at the ceiling, as Ben's typing hits warp speed.)

KIP – *For God's sake, stop that fucking racket you son of a bitch! It's happening all over again!*

 (Suddenly it stops, and Kip drops weakly into a chair... a few beats of silence, then Vivian and Ben in orgasmic concert, cry out loudly, from the attic.)

FLAT OUT!

CHAPTER ELEVEN

SETTING: The kitchen with round table, three weeks
after ACT TWO Scene Five.

AT RISE: Ben, in a white shirt, red tie and grey
jacket, is at the table with coffee and reading The New
York Times. Vivian sweeps in, dressed in a white skirt,
maroon silk blouse, with pearls and white jacket,
kisses Ben and pours some coffee.

BEN - Well, doesn't my brilliant, beautiful wife of the
Zeitgeist look all spiffy this morning. All dolled up
for…?

VIVIAN- Thanks, love. I'm to give my paper at the lunch
meeting of the Alpha & Omega Math and Physics Club.

BEN - On what, pray tell?

VIVIAN - Three levels actually --how Morgan invented
his method of removing decoherence from macro objects,
the status of his Nobel process and if you don't mind,
I want to go into our great adventure of living to the
hilt Morgan's one great story, enacting our sides of
the polarity with all our might… (a beat) Don't you just
love the picture of us in that hilarious struggle to
escape the deadly Newtonian lock-box…and then tell them
how you worked up The Leftover Brother, discovered that
both scientific and artistic breakthroughs came from
the same matrix in the Implicate Order and how Morgan,
though he could no longer invent at the quantum level

he could and *did* channel his genius to his artist son.
And how that revelation to Morgan started *his* emergence
from catatonia, and led to his release to us to his old
attic lair, where it all began.

BEN - Lord, the whole loaf! Sure doll, have at it.
Where are you holding forth?

VIVIAN - Downtown Hilton - they will tape it I think
and I want to show it to Morgan but I want *you* there!

BEN - Sure! How is Morgan doing since he settled in
from the asylum? I haven't seen him much since I've
been back to work at my day job with my broker. I got a
good working draft of LOB.(a beat - he holds up the
pages.) I'm shutting it down, to let my subconscious
fill up with grist, coast while I muck around the macro
world of investments on the bubble of Wall Street.

VIVIAN - Better every day. Not the old house-on-fire
magician/seer but more alert by the hour. He is *so*
appreciative how you got into the asylum, undercover,
and worked with him to get him started out of his black
hole. That was a loving, heroic thing you did Ben, for
your Dad, going out there, working your play, acting
crazy, not knowing if they would ever release you,
based on those symptoms.

BEN - It was tricky, walking the tightrope across that
absurd institutional chasm. It took all my energy to
write myself into Seventh Heaven, then to write and
wrestle on the page, to get Kip out there in my place.
So what does Dad do all day?

VIVIAN - Small things. Baby steps, back maybe to his near seer status, keep him busy. Plus, since he can't get back to Princeton to see his old friends and tell them about his decoherence coups de grace, I hooked up a speaker phone arrangement so he can talk with them at the Institute for Advanced Study.

BEN - Really! How thoughtful sweetheart. Who does he speak with?

VIVIAN - John Wheeler mostly, who's amazing, was there with Niels Bohr, Einstein, Godel, in '42, now ninety six and still teaching. John Nash calls and gives Morgan support to fight the demons. Freeman Dyson, Hugh Everett are there as well. They are all really happy for Morgan and his decoherence triumph, his shot at a Nobel.

BEN - Well I'll be. I'd love to be a fly on the wall when *they* all get together. Who is Hugh Everett? What did he do?

VIVIAN - Hugh is teaching there now but in '57, as a student of John Wheeler, he proposed perhaps the most radical solution to Schrodinger's Cat paradox at the time: his multiverse, stating that contrary to the uncertainty theory, where you have all the possible worlds in the quantum, if you look at one, it collapses into hard copy, but the other worlds remain in potentia. But multiverse says they *also* exist as distinct worlds, simultaneously and parallel with the collapsed one. Which means the universe is constantly bifurcating each quantum instant, spinning off into infinite numbers of quantum universes.

(Ben fixes his erotic eye on Vivian's hips and legs, and runs his hand up under her skirt)

BEN - I love it when you talk dirty. *Please* tell me you *do* have time for a quickie right here on this table?

VIVIAN -(laughing - pushes his hand away) Ben, you're a *sex fiend!*. It's only been an hour since - plus, we agreed, no more quickies for us, only longies. I'm off!

BEN - Oh, did I tell you, Kip just called for about the twentieth time from the Seventh Heaven Mental Hospital and Spa. He's really having a rough time, is riled at us for having him committed after his breakdown, and is telling the shrinks he is being vaporized by some quantum voodoo magic. He wants to know if you can stop by for awhile, and see what you can do to get him out of there and back to the Coast.

VIVIAN - Oh, I don't know, Ben. You know what happens when we get close, the Demon Ditz in me starts raging in her cage. I might lose control.

BEN - It would be the humane thing to do Vi and will give you a workout in resisting the Ditz.

VIVIAN - Well, OK, I'll stop by on my way to the luncheon. So you'll be there my love, noonish?

BEN - Wild horses darlin'.

CHAPTER TWELVE

SETTING: The room in the mental hospital where Morgan had been, which is now Kip's room.

AT RISE: Kip, languishes on the bed, appears depressed, thin and disheveled, sees Vivian enter and sit down in a chair across the room. He struggles to rise but falls back on the bed.

KIP – Good Lord, Vi, you finally came! I've been calling and calling. Where have you *been* these past three weeks? I'm about to go over the edge!

VIVIAN – I've been… busy…getting myself in shape.

KIP – Why did you leave me like that? We were getting along fine when you pulled the plug and went back to Ben.

VIVIAN – You made me mad. I thought that when I went out and dragged you back to my bed, you could keep up with me and not turn into a wimp.

KIP: A *wimp?*-- just because I wanted a time-out from our fucking marathon? I told you it wasn't personal, only temporary. You women don't know what it takes for a guy to be ready all the time. All you have to do is lie there and spread your legs.(a beat – stares at her) Look at you, you've gone back to your egghead ways, right?

VIVIAN - Yes. In fact I'm on my way to give a talk to other eggheads on the progress of Morgan's Nobel quest and the work Ben is doing on his experimental play, and how he has helped his father get well again. (a beat) Ben says that you have been calling, that you were feeling really bad?

KIP - *Yes!* Much worse than when they picked me up at the house, and way beyond where I was out on the Coast. How could Ben have sent me here? I needed his help and he abandoned me.

VIVIAN - You're kidding. It was payback in part for you sending *him* out here. Plus you were a wreck.

KIP - *You did all that Vi!* I just watched in amazement. And then that afternoon when Ben's typing started driving me nuts and I started getting… (a beat - sitting on the edge of the bed, thinking - a light comes on) Wait a minute. You said Morgan had lost the power to wax me. I'll bet Morgan somehow passed that power to Ben, and he's using his writing to keep up the attack on me? My god, *that's it!* Jesus, this is spookier than what happened in Laguna. That's what's happening Vi, *isn't it?*

VIVIAN - I don't know anything about that.

KIP - *You damn well do!* I can see it in your face, hear it in your voice. For God's sake Vivian if that's it, and Ben has taken over from Dad's attack on me, can't you get him to stop? I've been punished enough for standing up you and Dad at the church. Just call off the hounds and let me get back to California and I won't bother you all anymore. This whole thing has been a total fucking nightmare.

VIVIAN - Morgan can't help you as you know. Ben, not admitting he's doing it to you, can't help you either. As of this morning, he has shut down work on the play.

KIP- Then do something else Vi. *Please*! (a beat - holds up his hands and arms) Look at me. I'm diminishing as we speak. I'm losing weight, look like a ghost. I keep telling the shrinks about what Morgan did to me, used me as a goddamn lab rat for his quantum gig and they say, "sure - right" and double up on my meds. You have to tell them it's true, and that Ben is picking up Morgan's beat and doing the same thing. Morgan is looking to nail a Nobel prize and Ben maybe hit play, for what they *did* and *are doing* to me! I can't hold on much longer. You all are *family* for Christ's sake!

    (Vivian squirms in her chair, as the Ditz mode starts up. She walks over to the bed, stares at Kip who's desperation is plastered all over his face)

VIVIAN - I'll talk to the doctors. (a beat as she looks up and to the right as if hearing a voice)There *is* one other way that might work to get you out of here and on the road home. It has to do with another aspect of quantum mechanics. But it's a long shot.

KIP - Dear God, not that quantum crap again. But give it to me, I'm desperate!

VIVIAN - In the generic view of particle physics, out
of all available worlds sub-atomic wise, when one is
looked at, it collapses into hard copy, and the others
remain phantoms. In another view, they *don't* but are
also realized and exist beside to the world we chose.

KIP - Parallel universes? Yeah, I saw that on Star Trek
once. So what?

   (Vivian struggles to keep from jumping into bed with
Kip, has to hold onto the bed rail)

VIVIAN - Well, it's been reported that there are about
seven parallel worlds existing around us so that in
times of extreme danger, when a person is under severe
stress in one world...

KIP - Like I am now...

VIVIAN - Yes and if they concentrate, gather all their
energy and intention, rage or great anger, like Morgan
had at you at our wedding, they could cause what they
call sidestepping, so you "step out" of the dangerous
world, and into a more benign, less violent one. It's
worth a try.

KIP - What do I do?

   (Vivian takes a deep breath, reaches across the bed,
holding on to the headboard for ballast, pushes Kip
back down on the bed)

VIVIAN - Focus, gather all your anger from any source,
at being here, at Morgan, Ben, me if needed, for what
part we played in getting you so fucked up. Then
project the picture of being in the surf, sunup, at

Laguna Beach, running with the gorgeous love of your life into the rising sun, then falling on her and making wild love on the sand and you both have a huge climax! Go *flat out* with this! Just hold on to that picture as hard as you can!

(Kip lies back on the bed, closes his eyes, as his face contorts for five beats, -- then comes to.)

KIP - Damn, it didn't work. I'm still here. What now?

(Vivian lunges away from Kip, shakes her head, grabs her purse, heads for the door)

VIVIAN - Jesus, that was close. (a beat) Just keep it up, don't quit. Keep pushing at the edge of the envelope that holds the pictures of what is waiting for you on Laguna Beach, the sun, the surf, the good life with your main squeeze, how badly you want to be out of here, and use your rage at us as your jet fuel. It's your only hope Kip. Just do it, *damn it*!

(At the door Vivian turns to see Kip straining, and starting to glow a dull red-- then she is gone)

CHAPTER THIRTEEN

SETTING: The kitchen with round table as before.

AT RISE: Late afternoon of the same day as in ACT TWO Scene Six. Ben is at the table typing on the manuscript of The Leftover Brother. Vivian enters, stands, until Ben sees her, stops typing, and stares back at her.

VIVIAN - Genius at work? (a beat - Ben still stares.) What?

BEN - Lord, whatever you've been doing, they ought to bottle it. You look *ravishing!* There's is a purple aura around you--the color of the goddesses.

VIVIAN - They didn't bottle it but they did tape it.(a beat - she holds up the DVD disc) By the amount of smoke coming off those pages, I'd guess you're back in the LOB hot zone.

BEN - You bet darlin'- almost home, by the muses. Tell me all about your class A day.

   (Vivian goes to the sink, fixes a drink, walks around the table, speaking as she orbits.

VIVIAN - It was something special. But first tell me what got you going again on LOB?

BEN - Well, doll, I was half way out the door, to your gig, when I heard voices upstairs.

VIVIAN – Morgan had visitors from Princeton?

BEN – Way better, hon. Get this. I went up there and John Wheeler had put together a presentation, to review what had happened in the years since Einstein did Special and General Relativity using Michio Kaku's book Einstein's Cosmos, and the advances in quantum physics and was using Dad's new advance on cutting down decoherence in the macro world as the center piece. Morgan gave the session a full blow-by-blow description of how he had pulled out the picture from our wild day at the church, to Kip's caper, and my work on LOB. They had even brought Einstein's blackboard from his office showing his last futile efforts in a jumble of equations to invent the theory of everything. They had some of Princeton's young lion physicists there. They videoed it all and will send us a print.

VIVIAN – Morgan must have been floored and thrilled by it all. What else did they cover in the update?

BEN – What they hope to find when they crank up the Large Hadron Collider at Cern, the Higgs Boson, the "God particle", what dark matter and dark energy are, a fourth dimension, if supersymmetry exists, if cosmic inflation is active today. (a beat) They mentioned David Bohm and his rheomode language. Do you know about that?

VIVIAN – Yes, Bhom and his Wholeness and the Implicate Order where he verbalizes subject/ object language to more process words to help break through the wall of the Newtonian/Cartesian paradigm. Anybody else?

BEN - Hugh Everett was there and updated his parallel worlds idea. He discussed the trick of sidestepping from one world to another, when the heat in the kitchen gets too hot in one, you can, with the right amount of energy, jump the gap, and get out of a sticky wicket, into a safe haven. Do you know about that?

VIVIAN - Yes but not before this afternoon.

BEN - They closed with a picture of what Einstein was like in life, how he loved art as well as science to access, get glimpses of what he called "out yonder", where there exists this great cosmic construct, so foreign from anything in our world. How he loved to play Mozart violin sonatas, to get him into the zone of invention. Morgan said Einstein met Pirandello in Berlin, and told him with his plays, before Six Characters In Search of An Author, like Right You Are(If You Think So)were quantum solipsistic,cubist, relativistic theater, that they were kindred souls. All that from Princeton got me back in the zone. (a beat) Now, what about your dazzling day in the sun?

VIVIAN - It was fantastic. First, I stopped by to see Kip and got by a pretty hard siege of the Ditz.

BEN-(He picks up the manuscript of LOB and a pen) Let me read along here and edit the scenes as you lived them. Oh, by the way, Seventh Heaven called. Seems they have misplaced Kip. Just after you left him, they found his room empty, and just the scent of burnt flesh.

VIVIAN - Then it worked.

BEN - Apparently so - *and,* I had Kip finally figure out that before Morgan flamed out on his power to reshape atoms, he transferred it to me by a kind of osmosis to fuel the creative act of my writing LOB.

VIVIAN - Yes, he did. I was shocked he did as Kip has never been much of an intuitive dude -- but look who his father and brother are! And it was then we tried the sidestepping.

BEN (Ben makes notes on the script) But it didn't work there but did as you drove to the luncheon?

VIVIAN - Ben, it was the damnedest *thing!* I almost gave it up to the Ditz in the room, just barely got out of the hospital. In the car, I could *still* feel the wild woman pulling me back to him. She was pushing so hard to get out of my body, in a rage to have been denied, trying to break free to hook up with her man. I almost passed out, had to pull over, still fighting it when, at critical mass, she blew out of the top of my head and was gone!

BEN - Yes, gone, pulled out by Kip who had just blasted out of the crazy house, and had picked her up for their trip to the Coast.

VIVIAN - Or the Ditz was already in that world and yanked her hunk home to her love nest on the beach.

BEN - Right. Either way, they're back where they belong. Now the luncheon. (a beat - regards the script) See if I got it right.

VIVIAN - With the Ditz gone, I felt like a long
tethered eagle released to soar! I made the case for
you and Morgan, then began to rise metaphysically as my
archetype as teacher and scientist began to
constellate. I was on stage, able to participate in my
own ontological growth, became numinous. As an actor
whose character she owns, I went out of body to hover
over the audience, dealing the good stuff from the
Implicate to the Explicate Order. I felt you and Morgan
behind me urging me on in the rheomode. Then I came
back down to earth, a re-cast archetypal quantum woman,
to a full minute of applause!

BEN - Great! So why don't you go get a hot bath, read,
edit LOB for flow and structure so I can get a final
draft in the AM.(a beat) There's a great theatre space
in Manhattan we can rent and produce it in the Fall.
You acted in college, you can play yourself!

VIVIAN - Autumn in New York City. Can't beat that! I'll
dig out my Eleonora Duse book - The Mystic in the
Theatre and Stanislavski's - The Actor Prepares.

BEN - I'll fix dinner, bring it up, we can watch your
DVD, work on LOB. Maybe for a juicy encore we can…?

VIVIAN - Go flat out? Absolutely! Maybe Vivian #2,
before she took off to the Coast, left a residue of the
Ditz in me, so now with them gone, we can work on a
baby for us and Morgan to obsess over.(a beat - Vivian
fixes another drink, looks back at Ben, beaming at her
new Self.)

BEN - Good plan!

VIVIAN - Ben honey, hasn't our wild ride on the wave of quantum healing power been just thrilling? All that dross and neurotic crap of the reductionist Newtonian world of polarity has been torched, and we all, you, me, Morgan, and even Kip, have been to the belly of the beast, but like the phoenix, we've emerged... expanded and brighter, and now can help others make the same trip. I have hit the pinnacle of performance in my field, you have gone from nebbish to mensche, from dilettante to literary artist *par excellence!* Leftover brother...indeed. Once - maybe - but now you're Colorado Prime in my book! (a beat) And good *lord,* even the once Cretin Kip, in a supreme effort, has made the quantum leap into a parallel world that Morgan had predicted all along! I'll have to tell Morgan that and make his day!

BEN -And not in a burnt out space junkyard but into a California camp-out with his darling Ditz, (a beat) Before you go babe, let me ask you one thing. That time in the church Rector's office, eons ago. Do you have no memory of what we *really did,* when the Ditz fired out and took me for Kip?

VIVIAN - (laughing) I'll never tell. But why does what I say matter? As a card carrying quantum solipsist, you can make up whatever you want it to be out of the available quanta (a beat - holds up the LOB pages) Any ideas for the close on this? I've got a few I can give you when I get you upstairs.

BEN — Great! LOB is closing fast. I *do* have a picture of the final shot of what the Ditz and Kip might be doing about now, see them cavorting on Laguna Beach, buck naked, then falling to the sand, and making glorious love as did the couple in Tequila Sunrise!

VIVIAN — Yes, an excellent ending for those darling wild things. Just about what I told Kip to project for his escape from the house of horrors.

(Vivian exits, Ben turns as the last movement of a Mozart Violin Sonata begins playing softly from Morgan's lair)

BEN — *So...*is the cat dead or alive, a wave or particle? Or did we ever open Schrodinger's Box? Bottom line, is it even possible to know any kind of communicable truth while stuck, from birth, in the jailhouse of the either/or world of Newtonian physics while theorems in the quantum realm swirl around us in art and science? How close can the Greek *alethes* or Bohm's rheomode, get us to the truth, speak to us in Andre Gregory's argot of the heart, the language of the dancing bee that tells us where the honey is? Zen Master Yogi Berra, defines the essence of our spooky science, "When you come to a fork in the road, take it!" Godel gave us the key to the lock-box, with his liar's paradox, "A Cretin says, all Cretins are liars," It's up to *you all* to step up and choose your version of the truth! Am I a promising, *avant garde* playwright who has written the play, or plays, you have just seen? Or a literary lunatic on the loose, in deep delusion that he can write up "real" life? Sufi wisdom says, "When a pickpocket sees a saint, he can't see the halo, all he sees are the pockets."

(Ben enters the kitchen)

BEN - Do we have the courage to discard all *a priories* and as Fred Allen Wolfe and Pirandello say - create our worlds out of empty space - the way of quantum solipsism - the tree falling in the rain forest drill. Can we forever banish the Newtonian take that things are *already* things before we look at them? For St. Teresa of Avila, getting to Heaven *is* Heaven. The divine process in the subtext of this play *is* the divine comedy. Paradox is the platform to paradise and sublimity for the Morgans and Benjamins of this world.

(Ben serves up dinner from the cooker to plates on a tray, selects a bottle of wine. From above there's the sound of bath water running)

BEN - And now I repair to my re-born lady's chamber. But is she *there*, as the same amazing woman who's just had an out-of-body day, who's just given me the same come-hither look she'd given me...or Kip..take your pick, in the Rector's office? I hear the bath water running so the *probabilities* are building, the quantum proofs *pooling,* pro and con. And when I resume the quantum task of creating her anew, and gaze at her thru the steam of the bath, into the blur of the elusive electron, what truth will become unhidden *this* time - the lady or the tiger, the beauty or the crone? And later, locked up in love, on our red couch of Eros,we ultimately observe ourselves from above the position of the middle?

(Ben picks up the tray and heads upstairs. The running water stops, and is replaced by the closing chords of the Mozart Violin Sonata.)

THE END

———